shington Bulb Co.

Skagit Valley, Washington

Washington Bulb Co.

Brave Raven

GNASS PHOTO IMAGES
Bend, Oregon
(541) 383-5039
E-mail: office@gnassphotoimages.com
ISBN: 1-59975-645-5
ISBN 13: 978-1-59975-645-5
©2001 Brave Raven Books

Design: Principia Graphica

Cover photo: Washington Bulb Co.

Printed in Singapore

1 2 3 4 5 6 7 8 9

Spring Magic

The Tulips of Skagit Valley

by Rusty Middleton

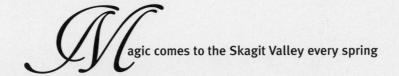

*M*agic comes to the Skagit Valley every spring

Gradually at first, and then often in a rush, the gentle earth tones of deep forest greens set against hues of tan and brown give way to striking ranks of reds, purples, whites and yellows. Already beautiful, the valley suddenly fills with color. The tulips have come into bloom.

At a distance the fields of flowers seem to create a kind of living watercolor. The edges blend and merge into one another like an artist's busy palette. But what the eye drinks in, the mind struggles to absorb. How can there be so much intensity on such an impossible scale?

Visitors often stand amazed, gazing at hundreds of acres awash in color. Yet these dazzling, expansive fields are simply a host of single flowers. In the end, it is the miracle of the individual tulip that awes us most.

The smooth, cool petals feel like satin or velvet. The lovely chalice shape manages to be both sensuous and elegant. And the colors seem to glow, to radiate from within. Indeed, you don't just admire a tulip, you want to caress it. Like a compelling work of art, these flowers somehow bypass the brain and go directly to our soul. "They make me feel peaceful," is a comment often made by visitors to the Skagit Valley Tulip Festival when they see the flowers.

Passion for tulips, in fact, has driven people to stake fortunes on an individual rare bulb. Once the tulip market even deflated the entire Dutch national economy. They are known to have inspired art, poetry and romance. For almost a thousand years, tulips have claimed a very special place in our hearts.

The Skagit Valley Tulip Festival

If you take a single flower and multiply it by hundreds of thousands; place those hundreds of thousands onto 1,500 acres or so of farmland and several spectacular display gardens; then place all this intense color in a beautiful valley surrounded by verdant mountains; then fill the valley with events, attractions and visitors from around the Northwest and the world; you will have only one thing, the Skagit Valley Tulip Festival.

Visitors to the family-oriented festival are treated to three weeks of fun events such as a salmon barbecue, bike and foot races, and a large street fair among many others. Plus they get very special experience with the flowers. During the Tulip Festival visitors can actually meander the fields through row upon row of near surreal color. Here you can get a sense of the texture and smell of the soil and a feel for the climate (perhaps including rain) that produces the greatest crop of tulips in America. In addition, several display gardens provide enchanting tours that showcase not just the tulips but also the many varieties of daffodils, iris and lilies also grown in the Skagit Valley. These spectacular gardens do much more than show off the flowers. They educate visitors on how to plan and develop their own gardens. These are places to investigate new varieties and visualize your own arrangements. The display gardens are especially useful to those with limited mobility.

The entire Festival experience goes far beyond simply admiring the flowers. Here you can see, feel, smell, and understand tulips and other bulbs from both the gardener's and the grower's perspectives.

TULIP TROLLEY

Tulip Town, Skagit Valley Bulb Co.

Roozengaarde, Washington Bulb Co.

Roozengaarde, Washington Bulb Co.

Tulip Town, Skagit Valley Bulb Co.

Behind the Flowers

The Tulip Festival is a celebration of the beauty of flowers but also a show of pride in success. Those magnificent springtime fields are the products of hundreds of years of accumulated wisdom, business acumen and plain hard work. As you stroll through the wonderland of color, it's sometimes hard to remember that this is very much an industry.

Skagit Valley's position as the major U.S. producer of bulbs is no accident. Its success is the happy result of European tulip farmers searching for and finding the near-perfect combination of climate and soil to grow bulbs in America. So, not only are the flowers here, but so are the people who have spent their lives growing them. Carrying the lore of generations of tulip farming with them, several families of Dutch farmers immigrated to the Skagit Valley during the 20th century. Pioneering Skagit tulip growers such as the DeGoede, Lefeber, and Roozen families experimented with different varieties, struggled with fluctuating market conditions, and patiently laid the foundation of what today is the largest bulb producing area in the U.S. and one of the largest outside Holland. The communities of Mount Vernon and LaConner were built in large part on the success of the farming and bulb industries that grew up in the valley. Thus the Skagit Valley bulb industry now sits at the apex of years of trial and error and refinement of bulb growing that has flourished for hundreds of years in Europe.

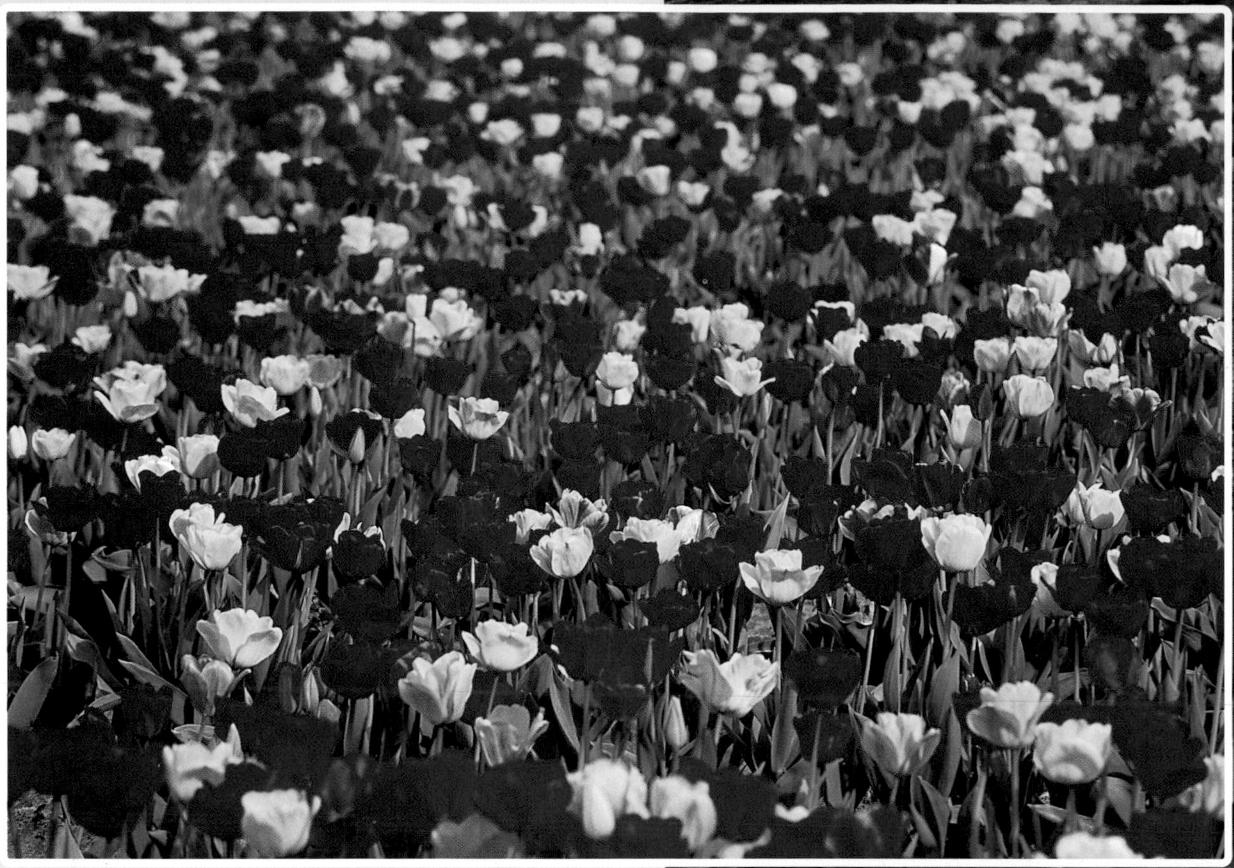
Lefeber Bulb Co.

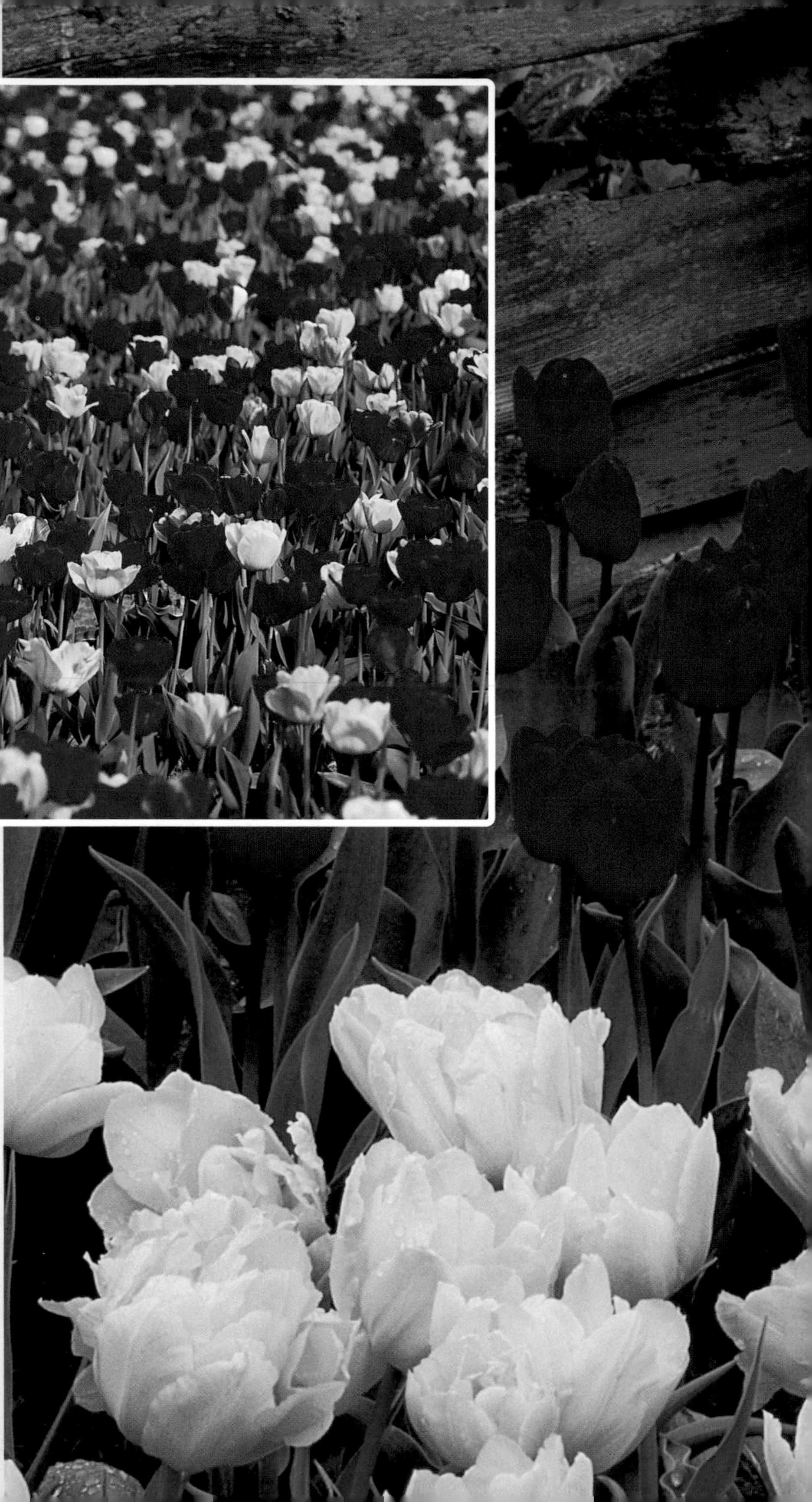
Roozengaarde, Washington Bulb Co.

The Industry Today

Cut flowers from tulip, iris, lily and daffodil bulbs now make up about half the valley's bulb industry. Flowers intended for the cut flower market are clipped while still encased in their tight green chrysalis of petals. Like small miracles, the green buds unfold after a few days in an explosion of radiant color when exposed to warmer temperatures and water. Grown both in fields and greenhouses, Skagit Valley cut flowers are shipped overnight across the U.S. almost year round.

Bulbs are a different business. Depending on weather and growing conditions, sometime in late spring special machines begin cutting the tops off the blooming flowers just before they pass their peak (sometimes to the horror of visitors who don't understand what is happening). This isn't spitefulness, it's more of a timely rescue. The petals, for all their delicate loveliness, are actually dangerous producers of plant disease when they fall on the lower leaves and begin to decay.

Cutting the blooms (known as topping) also helps to redirect the plant's energy into producing a bigger and better bulb. After topping, the bulbs are left in the ground until midsummer. Then they are extracted by machine, sorted for size and quality and shipped to marketers around the nation. Much of this business is done from orders placed over the phone and the internet.

Tulips are now appreciated and cultivated around the world. While Holland remains the world's largest tulip grower, Japan, England, Canada, and the U.S., among others, also have active tulip growing industries.

Over time, the tulip and bulb industry has adapted to changing conditions and markets, but admiration of the flowers has remained constant through the centuries.

A Brief History of Tulips

Even though we usually associate the history of tulips with Holland, they actually originated in the region between the eastern Mediterranean and the far reaches of China. Today it is considered extinct in the wild, perhaps because it has been so popular for so long. Images and artistic renderings of tulips have appeared on a twelfth century bible, in early Christian and Islamic art, and even in a painting depicting the Emperor Shah Jahan, builder of the Taj Mahal.

Tulips began to take on exalted status, and far greater value, when they became the court flower during the reign of Sultan Suleiman (1491-1566) of Turkey. Suleiman's son, Selim, is reputed to have initiated the first tulip rush by ordering up to 50,000 at a time for the royal gardens. The popularity of tulips reached its zenith in Turkey from 1703-1730 during the Lale' Devri or Tulip Period. At that time, the buying or selling of tulips outside the capital was banned on pain of exile.

Tulips made their way to Europe when a Flemish diplomat sent some bulbs home from Turkey in the middle 1500s. They quickly became the rage all across Europe, particularly in the Netherlands. In one bizarre three-year period from 1634-1637, tulips became the source of wild speculation. This brief era, known as tulipmania, saw fantastic sums exchanged for single bulbs on the gamble that they could be sold for even more. Like a pyramid scheme, it all came crashing down and the Dutch government finally stepped in to regulate sales. Today, after more than 400 years, the tulip industry still occupies a major niche in the Dutch economy.

rowing Your Own Bulbs

Raising tulips is easy. In general, you simply need to avoid exposing the bulbs to water-logged soil and frost, but there are numerous variations and exceptions according to climate and soil conditions. The best source of instructions for individual varieties comes from the growers and/or sellers. Skagit Valley growers supply precise instructions for each type of bulb they sell.

After you've enjoyed the flowers, cut off the past-peak blooms, but leave the foliage. Then just let the plant die down naturally, and the new bulbs will begin to develop. Six to eight weeks after topping, dig up the bulbs and store them with adequate ventilation and away from temperature extremes. Replant in the fall. Information on ordering Skagit Valley bulbs appears on the flap of the back cover.

With the astonishing array of tulip varieties available, choosing bulbs may actually be harder than planting them. The varieties seem endless. Out of about 80 basic species there are now thousands of possibilities. Varieties range from the simple cup shaped single color flowers to exotic, fringed, multicolor types that have taken anywhere from 14 to 20 years to develop. Some hybrids are better adapted to colder climates. In spite of the time and expense involved, new varieties are constantly being created and brought to market. Growers in Holland, where most new varieties come from, have recently introduced a new tulip called the Skagit Valley. It features white petals, with a soft pink blush, edged in purple. The Skagit Valley tulip is available from all Skagit Valley growers. Whatever the choice, once in the garden, tulips become the bright harbingers of spring adding character and elegance to flower beds and floral arrangements.

In the Skagit Valley, you can bring your family for a unique personal experience with the flowers and get to know the people, the communities and the environment that created the annual magic of tulips in spring.

Fishing boats in Anacortes

Ariel view of La Conner

5

Anacortes

Mount Vernon

La Conner

5

Seattle

Washington

5

Old Town Grainery in Mount Vernon

Downtown La Conner